Have you ever had a hard time solving a puzzle? Sometimes you need to think creatively. You need to think in a different way. This is called thinking outside the box.

Try the games and puzzles in this book. You'll need some materials first. You may want to get these things ahead of time.

- paper
- pencil
- toothpicks
- game pieces or counters, such as checkers, buttons, or coins
- **YOUR IMAGINATION!**

Here is a box that has been turned into a house. Can you draw it without lifting your pencil or going over any line twice? See if you can do it before you turn the page and look at a solution.

Do you need a hint? Don't start by drawing the box. Try going outside the box!

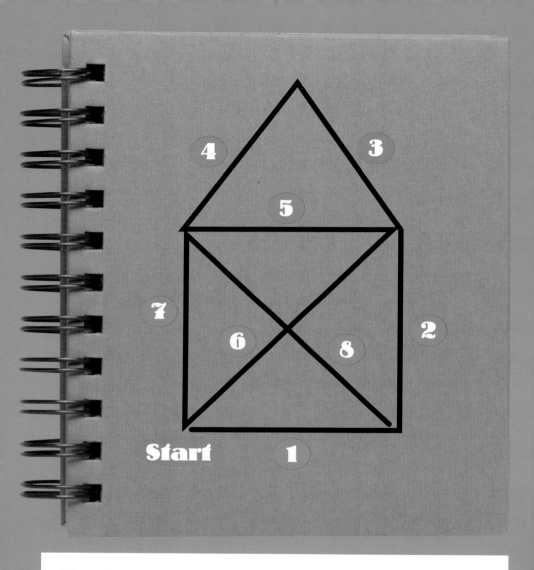

Here's one way to solve the puzzle. The numbers show the order in which to draw the lines. Try to find some other solutions, too.

How Many Boxes?

How many squares are in the box above?

If you see only nine squares, keep counting.
Turn the page to check your answer.

Did you count 14 squares? The colored lines show how to find them.

Magic Squares

4	9	2
3	5	7
8	1	6

Now you can use the same box for number magic!

- Add up the numbers in each of the three rows.
- Add up the numbers in each of the three columns.
- Add up the numbers in the two diagonals.

What do you notice?

The numbers add up to 15 every time!

People have played with magic number squares for hundreds of years. Benjamin Franklin liked to invent new magic squares. You can, too. Design a new magic square using the same numbers, 1 through 9, but put them in a different order.

For this puzzle you need two pennies and one nickel. On a sheet of paper, draw five boxes in a row. Then arrange the coins like this.

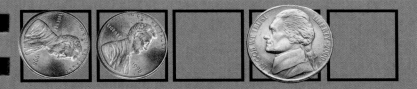

Move the coins to make this new pattern. The trick is you can only slide a coin one square at a time or jump over a different coin.

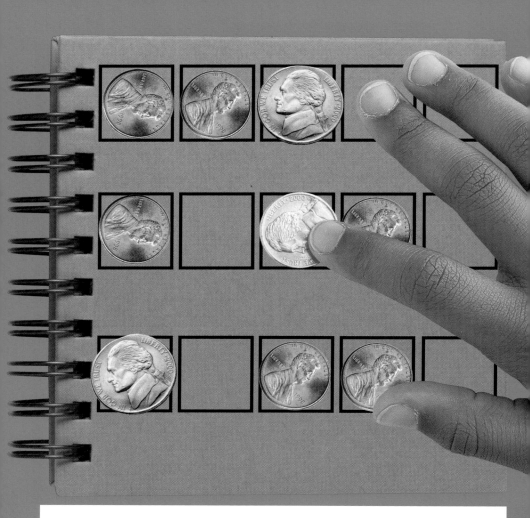

Did you figure it out?
Here's one way.

- Slide the nickel left.
- Jump over the nickel with the penny.
- Slide the nickel left.
- Jump over the nickel with the other penny.
- Slide the nickel left.

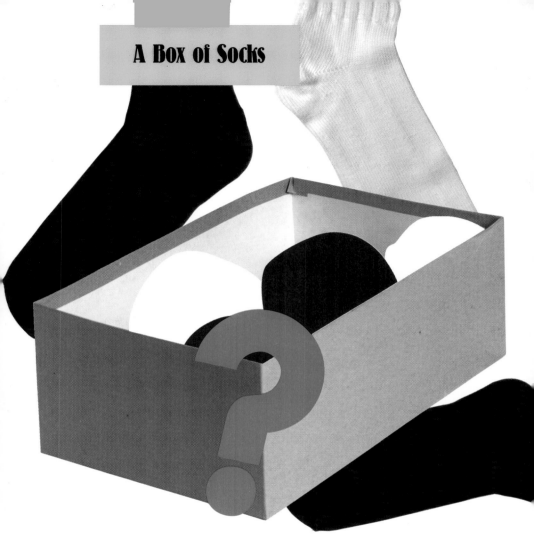

A Box of Socks

Imagine a box filled with six black socks and six white socks. If you take out one sock at a time, how many socks would you need to take out to be sure to find a matching pair?

Predict the answer. Then check your answer with a friend!

ANSWER: Three

Ask a friend to write a secret number between 1 and 100 in a box.

Then ask your friend, "Is the number closer to __ or to __?"

Each time, say different numbers in place of the blanks. Try to guess the number with as few questions as possible.

Each time you ask a question, make a tally mark in a box.

Keep asking questions until you figure out the mystery number. How many questions did it take until you found the answer?

Talk about how you could find the mystery number in the fewest guesses.

Draw a grid of ten dots by ten dots on a sheet of paper.

Try this game with a friend. For each turn, connect two dots with one line. Don't make diagonal lines. If the line you draw completes a box, write your initial in that box. Then take another turn.

16

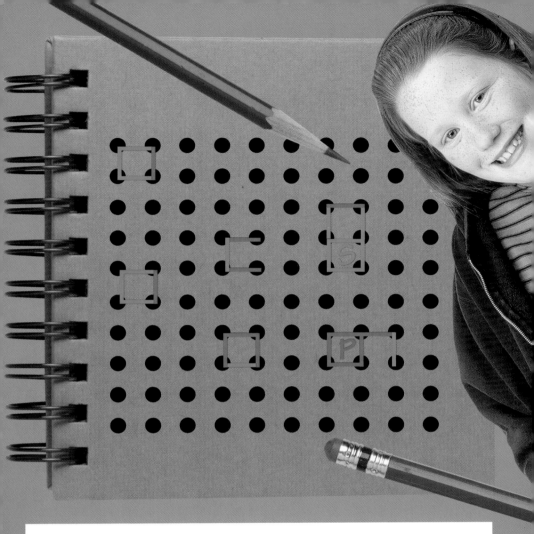

When all the dots have been connected,
count up the boxes each person completed.
Who captured the most boxes? Do you
think it matters who goes first or second
in this game? Why?

A Box of Bucks

Suppose someone in your family offers you these two choices.

1. Here is a dollar. Every day I will give you another dollar.

2. Here is a nickel. Every day I will double your money.

Which would you choose?

The dollar-a-day deal sounds pretty good, but look at this chart.

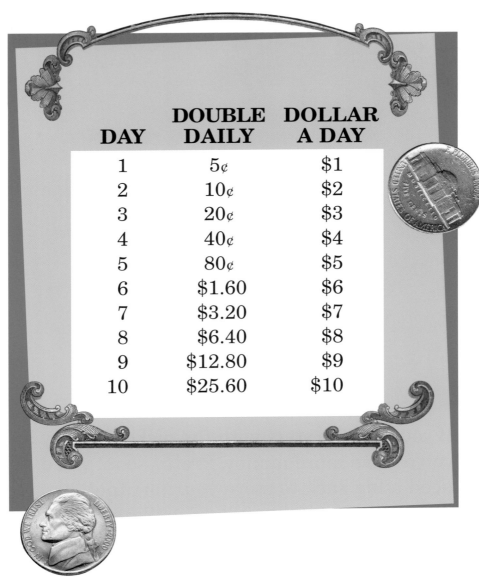

DAY	DOUBLE DAILY	DOLLAR A DAY
1	5¢	$1
2	10¢	$2
3	20¢	$3
4	40¢	$4
5	80¢	$5
6	$1.60	$6
7	$3.20	$7
8	$6.40	$8
9	$12.80	$9
10	$25.60	$10

If you chose to start with the nickel, by Day 9 you'd have more money. Pretty soon, you'd need a big sack to store your fortune!

Toothpick Trick

Get a box of toothpicks. Take six toothpicks out of the box.

How can you turn six toothpicks into twelve without breaking them in half?

21

Think outside the box! Use Roman
numerals.

Make up more puzzles using Roman
numerals. Here is a chart to help you.

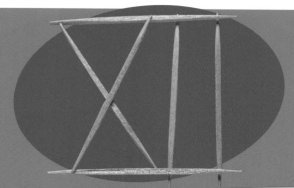

NUMBER	ROMAN NUMERAL
1	I
2	II
3	III
4	IV
5	V
6	VI
7	VII
8	VIII
9	IX
10	X
11	XI
12	XII

What's in the Box ?

Imagine that there are three closed boxes. One box contains books only. One box contains toys only. One box contains both books and toys. All the boxes are mislabeled.

How could you figure out what is in each box by opening only one box and removing only one item? Don't forget to "think outside the box"!

erfly, "I was not always
a caterpillar I was fuzzy
t look very special.
I came out of my
these beautiful wings of
aps if you spin yourself a
ave beautifully colored
merge."

erfly moved away from Bullfrog. She
float around the flowers. Her
ful wings fluttered through
pped at first one flow
appeared to
Soon
ay.

ANSWER: Pull one thing out of the box labeled **Books and Toys.** Since the label is wrong, the box contains either books or toys, not both. If you pull out a book, then you know that this is the **Books** box. Then, the books and toys must be in the box labeled **Toys,** and the toys are in the box labeled **Books.**